THE WOMAN WHO HEARD THE SUN

The New York Times

THE WOMAN WHO HEARD THE SUN

AND OTHER TRUE STORIES OVERLOOKED BY HISTORY

WRITTEN BY
AMISHA PADNANI

TEN SPEED YOUNG READERS
AN IMPRINT OF TEN SPEED PRESS
CALIFORNIA | NEW YORK

CONTENTS

INTRODUCTION

When I was a kid, I loved listening to other people tell stories about themselves—especially when they made me see the world in a new way. That's one of the reasons why I became a newspaper journalist. My job is to ask questions, listen closely, and share what I learn. I get to write about people's lives—what they care about, what they've been through, and how they've made a difference.

The section of the newspaper where I work is called Obituaries. An obituary is a story about someone who has died. It's a way to remember them, celebrate what they did, and show how their life mattered. Some of these people are well-known—like presidents who helped create important laws, athletes who broke records, and musicians whose catchy songs made us dance. Others aren't famous, but they still changed the world in important ways that sparked imagination—like the woman who created the sock puppet.

But after some time on the Obituaries desk, I started noticing a pattern. Most of the people we wrote about were men—especially men with a lot of money or power. Many of them were white.

Where were the women? The people of color? The members of the LGBTQ community? The people with disabilities? Where were the people who had changed history in quieter ways?

As a daughter of Indian immigrants, I wanted to see more stories that reflected the real world—and people who looked like me. So I started searching through old newspapers to find who had been left out. I discovered that *The New York Times* had never written an obituary about Major Taylor, the first Black world champion cyclist. Or Regina Jonas, the first woman rabbi. Or Ruby Payne-Scott, a scientist who helped us understand that the sun makes sounds.

I started talking to some friends, and we came up with an idea: What if we were to write the stories that should have been told all along?

That's how Overlooked began. Overlooked is a project that honors amazing people who were left out of the newspaper—and ignored throughout history—simply because someone didn't think their stories mattered.

But they do matter.

This book tells the stories of eighteen people whose creativity, courage, and curiosity helped shape the world we live in today.

As you read, I hope you'll ask yourself: Who else deserves to be remembered? Whose stories still need to be told?

Annie Edson Taylor (1838–1921) was an American schoolteacher who became the first person to survive going over Niagara Falls in a barrel, a feat she accomplished on her sixty-third birthday, October 24, 1901.

ANNIE EDSON TAYLOR

ONE WOMAN. ONE BARREL. ONE BIG WATERFALL.

Most people celebrate their birthdays with cake and candles. Not Annie Edson Taylor. For her sixty-third birthday, she wanted to do something no one had ever done: go over Niagara Falls—in a barrel—and live to tell the tale.

Niagara Falls is no ordinary waterfall. It's an explosive, crashing beast of nature, perched on the border between the United States and Canada. Water tumbles from a cliff as tall as a sixteen-story building and pounds into the river below with a thunderous roar that shakes the ground.

Nobody had ever attempted going over the falls in a barrel before. It was *way* too dangerous. But Annie pushed the scary thoughts from her head. There was no prize for doing this. Instead, she thought about piles of cash. She figured if she could pull off such a fearless, foolhardy feat, she was sure to become famous—and rich!

Annie was born on October 24, 1838, in the Finger Lakes region of New York. She had ten brothers and sisters. She didn't care much for dolls—she liked playing sports and reading stories about adventures. When she grew up, she became a teacher. But she always dreamed about having an adventure of her own.

Now that she was older, she realized there was no reason not to go for it. She had lost her job. She had no family, no children, no money. Sometimes Annie worried about how she would make ends meet. A big crowd was going to be near Niagara Falls in 1901 for the famous World's Fair—where countries from around the globe would showcase achievements in science, technology, culture, and art. If all those people saw what a daredevil she was, then she might even become a celebrity.

She designed her own barrel. First she drew a diagram. Then she made a tiny model out of cardboard and string. She brought it to a barrel-making shop and picked out every single piece of wood for the real barrel herself. Finally, it was done. It wasn't perfectly round—it was bumpy and shaped a bit like a football, less than three feet in the middle and skinny at the top and bottom. To keep it steady in the rushing water, workers wrapped it with ten metal bands. They also put an anvil—a heavy weight—at the bottom to keep it upright. Inside, Annie added pillows for padding and a seatbelt to hold her in place.

She chose to go over the Horseshoe Falls, the biggest of the three falls at Niagara. A small group of friends helped her set everything up—she didn't do it alone. And she spent days preparing. She even sent the barrel over the falls first with a cat inside. (Don't worry—the cat survived with just a tiny cut on its head!)

Annie Edson Taylor crossing the Niagara River on a plank with the falls in the distance.

“PEOPLE CALLED HER “THE QUEEN OF THE MIST” AND “THE GODDESS OF WATER.””

Word had gotten out about what she was planning to do, and crowds gathered to watch. Some people tried to talk her out of it, warning her that it was too dangerous. But Annie was determined.

She took off her hat and her coat, climbed into the barrel, and closed the lid. It was pitch-black inside. It smelled like wood and river water. She was nervous. But she was also ready for the ride of her life.

“I felt as though I were being suffocated,” she said later. She squeezed her eyes shut and reminded herself that she was brave.

As it got closer to the waterfall, the barrel swerved and swooped. Inside, Annie was tossed about like a sock in a washing machine—banging into the sides, her head spinning, water sloshing at her feet. It was so loud, she couldn't even hear herself scream. The barrel paused for a moment at the top of the waterfall, then, as Annie put it, “made the awful plunge.” It was like riding a roller coaster in nature, only riskier.

Then—*smack*! The barrel hit the water and disappeared beneath the surface. Would it ever come back up?

People onshore held their breath, eyes locked on the waves. At last, the barrel bobbed to the surface.

A rescue crew rushed out, pulled the barrel to land, and opened it up. Fresh air hit Annie's face. She was shaken, dizzy, and hugging a soggy pillow.

“Good God! She's alive!” one of the rescuers shouted.

A horn sounded. The crowd burst into applause, their cheers echoing over the roar of the falls.

Annie was famous for a little while. People called her “the Queen of the Mist” and “the Goddess of Water.” She wrote a book about her adventure and traveled around

THE DAREDEVILS OF NIAGARA

In 1901, Annie Edson Taylor was the first person to go over Niagara Falls in a barrel and survive, but hundreds of people have gone over the falls—both before and after her. Only sixteen of them survived. Sometimes they did it for adventure. Other times they did it by accident. In 1951, the government made performing stunts over the falls illegal, and anyone who was caught would be fined—up to thousands of dollars. Although that didn't always stop them.

Here are some of their stories.

1853 Three men were rowing a boat that flipped upside down. None of the men survived. Two of them tumbled over the falls immediately. The third, Joseph Avery, grabbed onto a tree root and held on for dear life. The next day, rescuers came and tried to get him into their boat, but he was thrown back into the water and hurtled down the falls. Today, a rock near the tree root is called "Avery's Rock."

1911 Bobby Leach was a stuntman for the circus. He said that anything Annie could do, he could do better. He chose a barrel made of steel and survived the tumble, but he spent six months in the hospital.

1928 Jean Lussier went over Niagara Falls in a giant rubber ball, thinking the rubber would help him float. The ball split apart—but he didn't. Later, he sold pieces of the ball to tourists.

1961 Nathan Boya was the first Black person to go over the falls, in a metal ball he called the "Plunge-O-Sphere." He was arrested. He later said he did it because he was heartbroken: He was supposed to go to Niagara Falls on his honeymoon, but the wedding never happened.

the country to tell people about it. She didn't make as much money as she'd hoped, but she did inspire other people to try their own daring stunts over the falls (not all of them were as lucky).

Annie showed the world that bravery doesn't have to look like a big, strong superhero in a cape. It can be seen in anyone—even a tough lady with gray hair, a heart full of courage, and a barrel full of hope.

Annie Edson Taylor and her friends making their way to Horseshoe Falls on the day of Annie's big adventure.

ALISON HARGREAVES

MOUNTAINEER, MOTHER, AND MUSE

Alison Hargreaves was standing on top of the world.

Literally.

It was May 13, 1995, and she had just reached the summit of Mount Everest—29,029 feet high. That's taller than a thousand school buses stacked on top of one another. Higher than the clouds. The sky felt close enough to touch.

She looked out at the snowy mountain peaks all around her, then pulled out her radio and spoke into it: "To Tom and Kate, my dear children, I am on the highest point of the world, and I love you dearly."

Alison had just made history. She was the first woman to climb Mount Everest all by herself—with no one to help, and no bottled oxygen. The higher climbers go, the thinner the air gets, which makes it harder to breathe. Most mountain climbers bring a tank of oxygen with them, but Alison wanted to prove that she didn't need extra air. She had spent years training her body—and her mind—for this.

Alison was born on February 17, 1962, in Derbyshire, England. As a little girl, she loved hiking with her family. Her bedroom walls were covered in posters of mountains. She didn't dream about being famous. She dreamed about climbing.

She started rock climbing when she was thirteen, and it wasn't just a hobby. A few years later, she moved on to mountains, practicing harder climbs and earning a reputation among other climbers for her skill and courage. But she noticed something: Most famous climbers were men. And they had teams of helpers to carry their gear.

She wanted to show that a woman could be just as fearless as anyone else. Maybe even more fearless.

"I think that women in general have to work harder in a man's world to achieve recognition," she said.

British climber Alison Hargreaves during her successful attempt to become the first woman to climb Everest unaided and without oxygen.

So she decided to do something no woman had ever done:

Climb Everest alone.

Climb Everest without oxygen.

Climb Everest as a mother.

She started her ascent from camp at four a.m. She carried the essentials herself—her tent, sleeping bag, food, and climbing gear. She moved slowly. Carefully. She counted her breaths. In, out, in, out. Ice crunched under her feet. Her fingers ached from holding the ropes. But she stayed focused, steady. She knew how to get through this. She knew how to be patient.

At one-thirty in the afternoon, she stepped onto the top of the world—and cried happy tears. The wind felt so cold on her face that it burned. Snow sparkled like crushed diamonds under her boots. The air was thin, and each breath was like sipping through a straw. But none of that bothered Alison. She felt her heart might burst—from joy, from pride, from love. It was like standing in one of the posters from her childhood bedroom. It was like standing in a dream.

Her family and friends were thrilled. Alison had just done something no other woman on Earth had done. But when she came home, the world didn't cheer—it questioned her. News reporters didn't ask how the world looked from the summit, or how she felt when she cried into the wind. Instead, they asked: "How could you have left your children behind? What if something bad had happened to you? Who would have taken care of them?"

Alison was shocked. Why didn't anyone ask those questions of the fathers who climbed?

Her children and her husband supported her—and her kids would grow up to be climbers themselves.

She knew she had nothing to apologize for.

And many people agreed. In fact, Alison became a hero to a new generation of girls and women who wanted to climb. She didn't just inspire them—she helped change what people thought mothers could do.

She once said: "If you are given two options, take the harder one because you'll regret it if you don't. At least if you take the harder one and fail, you'll have tried."

And Alison didn't fail.

She soared.

EVEREST: THE ULTIMATE CHALLENGE

Every serious climber has a dream: Conquer Mount Everest. Why? It's the tallest mountain on Earth, and reaching the summit is extremely difficult. For decades, climbers tried and failed. By the time Alison Hargreaves set her sights on Everest, most people who had made it to the top had teams of Sherpas—skilled guides—and other people to carry their gear. They needed a lot of items, including:

- High-energy foods like chocolate, nuts, dried fruit, and freeze-dried meals to prepare with hot water
- A tent, a sleeping bag, and a small stove
- Thick socks, mittens, boots, waterproof jackets, and thermal underwear and pants
- An ice axe, ropes, harnesses, a helmet, goggles, sunscreen, lip balm, a headlamp with extra batteries, bottled oxygen, and first-aid supplies
- Maps, a compass, and a radio for emergencies

Alison carried all of that herself—no bottled oxygen, no team. Only one person had ever done it before: Reinhold Messner, a man from Italy, in 1980. When Alison reached the summit in 1995, she proved that one woman, alone, could face one of the most dangerous places on Earth—and survive.

Portrait of African American cyclist and champion Marshall "Major" Taylor (1878–1932) seated on a bicycle, 1898.

MAJOR TAYLOR

WHO CYCLED PAST THE HATERS

Imagine riding so fast on a bicycle that no one can catch you—not even a car. More than a hundred years ago, that was Major Taylor, one of the fastest athletes on two wheels. When Major Taylor pedaled his bike, he could go faster than most cars could drive back then—about 35 miles per hour.

His real name wasn't actually Major—it was Marshall.

Marshall Taylor was born on November 26, 1878, in Indianapolis, Indiana. As a young boy, he worked for a cycle shop, and to bring in more customers, he would do bicycle tricks outside while dressed in a soldier's uniform. People gave him the nickname Major—which is a rank that some people in the Army achieve.

Major Taylor had legs of steel. They weren't really made of steel, but they might as well have been. His muscles were really strong.

And Major Taylor was determined. The shop owner was so impressed by his skills and strength that he entered him in a race. He was only thirteen years old, and he won by six seconds! From then on, all he wanted to do was race on his bicycle—feeling the wind whip across his face and the handlebars vibrate under his fingers, seeing trees and buildings pass by in a blur, and hearing the crowd's cheers turn to a distant hum behind him.

Major Taylor was Black—and back then, that meant he wasn't allowed to race in most places. In Indianapolis, only white riders could compete. That wasn't fair, but it was the rule. So he moved to Massachusetts, hoping for a better chance. He was allowed to race there, but people were still mean to him. They splashed him with freezing water that soaked his clothes and stung his skin. Sometimes he'd hear the crunch of a purposefully placed nail under his tire—then the sudden hiss of air escaping, forcing him to stop and start all over again.

"He had to be terrified," said Karen Brown-Donovan, his great-granddaughter, adding, "especially since he was the only person of color on the track."

> **NEWSPAPERS CALLED HIM "THE FASTEST MAN IN THE WORLD."**

Finally, Major Taylor decided to move to France, where life was different. There, people didn't treat him unfairly because of the color of his skin. Instead, they cheered him on.

"Major Taylor had a proud and confident identity in Europe and was not a crushed or threatened Black man," the historian Andrew Ritchie wrote in a book about Major Taylor.

When he raced through the streets of Paris, crowds went wild. Fans waved flags and shouted his name. Newspapers called him "the fastest man in the world." He was invited to race in cities across Europe, and he won again and again. For the first time, Major Taylor felt what it was like to be seen—not because of what he looked like, but because of his special talent.

He didn't have to look over his shoulder—he could just ride, heart pounding, legs burning, joy rising in his chest like a balloon. He even got another nickname: the Black Cyclone.

As Major Taylor grew older, people began to forget about him. He had raced so hard for so long, but he spent his final years alone. He died in 1932 in Chicago, Illinois, with little money. But his daughter never forgot. She saved his medals, trophies, and letters—because she knew the world would want to remember him someday.

Today, there are bike clubs named after him, and a statue of him stands tall in Worcester, Massachusetts. He showed the whole world that no matter what people said, he could be great—and he was.

Bicyclist Marshall "Major" Taylor poses for a portrait in 1906.

RALPH LAZO

WHO FOLLOWED HIS FRIENDS INTO HISTORY

Ralph Lazo looked out the train window, but he wasn't admiring the view. He was thinking about where he and his friends were heading—and he was terrified.

The train was rattling through the California desert. Everyone sat in silence. No one was laughing or joking like they usually did. No one even whispered.

They were all thinking about the same thing: They were going to a prison camp. Someplace no one should ever have to go.

Ralph was born on November 3, 1924, in Los Angeles, California. He lived near a neighborhood called Little Tokyo, named for a city in Japan because a lot of Japanese American families lived there. Ralph, who was Mexican American, became close with the kids who lived nearby.

At school, they were almost never apart. They played basketball and ate dinner at each other's houses. Ralph even started to learn to speak Japanese. "We developed this beautiful friendship," he later said.

But in 1942, when Ralph was seventeen, everything changed. One by one, his classmates disappeared. Their desks sat empty.

That's because after Japan attacked Pearl Harbor in Hawaii, the U.S. government made a shocking decision: More than a hundred thousand people of Japanese ancestry—mostly on the West Coast—were forced to leave their homes. They were sent to live in prison camps, far away from everything they knew.

Many of them were American citizens, just like Ralph. They'd been born in the United States. His friends, who were also teenagers, had done nothing wrong. But they were being treated like enemies.

Ralph couldn't believe it. Were his friends really being taken away just because of their race? That wasn't right.

"Who can say I haven't got Japanese blood in me?" he said. "Who knows what kind of blood runs in my veins?"

Mexican American student Ralph Lazo in a yearbook photograph from 1944. He pretended to be Japanese so he could be willingly interned with his friends.

The Manzanar War Relocation Center was one of ten camps where people of Japanese ancestry were imprisoned.

As he helped his friends get ready for their moves to the camp, he felt their pain and confusion. And then his heart spoke to him. It said: Go with them.

He told his father he was going to camp. At first, he didn't say what *kind* of camp. He didn't want him to worry. But he was going to Manzanar—one of ten internment camps that the government had set up in lonely, dusty parts of the country.

At Manzanar, in Owens Valley, California, life was harsh. The summers were scorching hot, the winters were freezing cold, and families lived in cramped spaces with barely any privacy. Everyone had to use open bathrooms and wait in long lines to eat terrible food. Tall fences surrounded the camp so no one could leave, and guards stood watch just in case they tried.

> **HIS KINDNESS GAVE PEOPLE STRENGTH.**

Ralph saw how broken his friends felt, so he tried to cheer them up. He played games with them. He told jokes to the little kids. He led a group of carolers at Christmastime. His kindness gave people strength.

Ralph stayed at Manzanar for about two years, until the government discovered his secret: that he wasn't Japanese, and that he didn't even have to be at the camp. But instead of punishing him, they shared his story with newspapers. They thought Ralph's story would make the camp—and the government—look good, even though the camps were unfair. Soon the world knew about the bighearted decision Ralph had made. He was sent overseas to serve in World War II, where he earned a Bronze Star for bravery.

After the war, Ralph kept fighting for justice. He helped students from Latino and other underrepresented communities go to college. He also spoke up for Japanese Americans who had been imprisoned and pushed the government to apologize.

But when reporters asked him to talk about himself, he usually refused.

"Please write about the injustice of the evacuation," he once said. "This is the real issue."

Ralph Lazo didn't go to the prison camp for attention or praise. He went because when you care about your friends, you don't look away—you show up. Even when you're scared.

Ralph Lazo, far right in the middle row, with his friends at Manzanar.

Sarah E. Ray in 1974 visiting a neighbor's house that had been burned down. She became a leader in her community.

SARAH E. RAY

WHO TOOK A RIDE TO JUSTICE

Sarah E. Ray beamed as she stepped onto the boat, her whole body tingling with excitement.

After going to college for a year, she'd made the decision to switch to secretarial school. She'd just graduated and she and her classmates were going on a trip to celebrate—to an amusement park called Bob-Lo Island near Detroit, Michigan. It was June 22, 1945. The sun was shining, the water sparkled, and seagulls squawked overhead. The dock buzzed with laughter and chatter.

Sarah and her friends took their seats and started talking about the games they'd play and the picnic they'd have once they got to the island. Waves splashed against the sides of the boat as if they were joining in the conversation. It was shaping up to be the perfect day.

But then something really upsetting happened.

A man who worked for the boat company marched up to Sarah and told her to get off. Just her. She was the only Black student in her class, and the company had a rule that Black people were not allowed to ride.

As the boat pulled away without her, Sarah's face burned with shame. She felt stunned and sad as her friends left her behind. But soon those feelings turned into something else: outrage. The color of her skin shouldn't matter. She had studied just as hard as everyone else. She deserved to be a part of the celebration.

"I was so angry," she said many years later. "Angry and hurt and humiliated and embarrassed before all these girls. To think that I'd spent months with these girls and all of a sudden, I'm different?"

Sarah picked up the phone and called the Detroit office of the NAACP, which stands for National Association for the Advancement of Colored People—a group that fights for the rights of Black Americans. Her voice shook as she told them what had happened.

They listened. And they took her case to court. Sarah felt a spark of hope. She wasn't alone anymore. Someone was fighting for her.

The NAACP argued that the boat company had broken Michigan's civil rights law, which said that businesses couldn't treat people differently just because of their race.

The company tried to wiggle out of it. They said that the law didn't apply to them because the boat went to an island in Canada. But the judges didn't buy it. They ruled that Bob-Lo Island was still part of Detroit, and that what had happened to Sarah wasn't just wrong—it was illegal.

This was nine years before the famous *Brown v. Board of Education* Supreme Court case that ended segregation in schools. And ten years before Rosa Parks refused to give up her seat on a bus in Alabama. That's why Sarah's case mattered so much: It helped lead the way in a bigger fight for justice.

Sarah was born near Chattanooga, Tennessee, but moved to Detroit hoping for more freedom and opportunity. She was disappointed to find that racism followed her there—but she didn't let it define her.

Sarah's win that day in court was bittersweet. Her chance to go to the amusement park was gone, and nothing could bring it back. But she used that moment—that anger, that energy—to keep fighting.

She and her husband started a neighborhood center called Action House, a safe place where Black children could play after school. Her real hope was to build an inclusive community where everyone was welcome.

Not many people knew what had happened on the boat that day. But Sarah never forgot. And thanks to the people who later shared her story, we don't have to forget either.

She was told she couldn't have a seat. So she stood up—tall and proud—for herself and for the generations that followed.

MOMENTS THAT MADE A MOVEMENT

In 1954, the Supreme Court made a huge decision in a case called *Brown v. Board of Education.* It said that schools for Black and white children had to be equal—because separate schools were unfair. Before that, many Black kids went to schools that were tiny, old, and falling apart, with cracked desks, broken chalkboards, and barely any books. Meanwhile, white kids got new buildings, fresh supplies, and full libraries. Imagine going to school every day knowing that your classroom was treated like it didn't matter. Like *you* didn't matter. *Brown v. Board of Education* changed children's lives.

A year later, in 1955, Rosa Parks refused to give up her seat on a bus to a white passenger in Montgomery, Alabama. Black people were forced to sit in the back or stand when the bus was full—even though they paid the same fare as white riders. But Rosa was tired. Her feet ached from a long day at work. When she refused to move, the driver called the police, and Rosa was arrested.

Her act of courage inspired thousands of Black people. They refused to ride the buses in a huge protest called the Montgomery Bus Boycott. Their fight led to the court case *Browder v. Gayle,* and the Supreme Court finally said that segregated buses were illegal.

The court case and Rosa Parks's arrest show how brave people have made the world a fairer place—and why standing up for what's right matters.

QIU JIN

WHO DREAMED OF A NEW CHINA

Qiu Jin (pronounced Chi-u Jin)* was born in Xiamen, China, on November 8, 1875 (some scholars say 1877). She quickly realized she was living in a man's world. Here, emperors ruled and women were silenced.

Women were not allowed to leave the home.

Women were not allowed to speak their minds.

Women were not allowed to choose whom they married.

Women were pretty much not allowed to do anything Jin wanted to do. She wanted to read books, but girls weren't allowed to go to school, so she found her own way—sneaking books meant for boys and reading everything she could. She believed that smart, strong women could help change the world.

Like most little girls at the time, Jin had to bind her feet. Binding means wrapping feet in cloth so tightly that you can barely walk. The idea is to make your feet look smaller, more dainty and ladylike. Every time Jin looked down at her aching bound feet, she felt trapped—like her body wasn't even hers.

When she grew up, she got married, even though it wasn't what she wanted. She was expected to stay at home, sew clothing, and serve her husband. Nothing more, nothing less.

Jin felt like the walls were closing in on her. Something had to change. When she was about twenty-eight years old, she made a bold choice: She sold her jewelry for money, left her husband, and traveled to Japan, where she could be herself.

In Japan, she went to school, and she met other people who also wanted women in China to have rights, like the right to go to school, have a job, and do whatever they wanted. Jin started playing with swords, drinking wine, and making bombs. She tied

---

* In China and other East Asian countries, last names are given before first names.

Qiu Jin with her hair tied back, wearing men's clothes and boots.

Qiu Jin holding a sword.

her hair back, slipped on men's clothes and boots, and looked in the mirror. Now she wasn't just someone's wife or daughter but someone who was choosing her own path.

After two years, she went back to China to share what she had learned with other young women. She started a magazine and wrote poems and essays about the China she dreamed of. She led other women to stand up against unfair gender roles. She expressed herself in fierce poems, writing:

My body will not allow me
To mingle with the men.
But my heart is far braver
Than that of a man.

Not everyone liked what Jin was saying. The empire she challenged was harsh and unforgiving. Speaking out was dangerous. Fighting back could cost you your life. But Jin refused to stay quiet. When she began planning a revolution to fight for change in China, the government found out.

Her friends rushed to warn her. They begged her to run away.

But she didn't.

She stood tall and proud. When the guards came, she didn't flinch. Her eyes blazed with courage. The government said she had to die for her beliefs. She was beheaded by imperial forces on July 15, 1907, becoming a revolutionary martyr. She was just thirty-one years old.

Even though she was gone, her courage had lit a spark. A few years later, the emperor's rule was overthrown. China began to change, and women began to speak out louder and dream bigger. Jin's bravery gave them someone to believe in—someone who showed that one voice can shake an empire.

Today, she is remembered as a hero. There are statues of her in China, and her poems are read in classrooms. She didn't get to see the changes she dreamed of, but because of her, they began. And today, girls across China grow up knowing her name—and knowing that their voices matter.

Molly Nelson, who later took the name Spotted Elk, in a portrait from the 1930 movie *The Silent Enemy*.

MOLLY NELSON

WHOSE DANCES TOLD STORIES

Molly Nelson loved to dance. But more than that, she wanted people to understand where her dances came from.

She was born on November 17, 1903, on Indian Island—the heart of the Penobscot (pronounced Puh-NOB-scott) Nation in Maine. She came from a big family—she had seven younger brothers and sisters—and though her real name was Mary Alice, everyone called her Molly.

Her family made and sold baskets to earn a living. Her mother wove them; her father gathered the materials. Money was hard to come by. But stories? Those were everywhere.

Molly wanted to know all of them. She did chores around the house, and in exchange, she asked elders to tell her legends—about animals, spirits, and the land her people had lived on for thousands of years. She soaked up everything she heard.

She also loved to perform. Her first time onstage, she danced an Irish jig in a school contest. By the time she was a teenager, she was earning dimes dancing for tourists. Sometimes she performed traditional dances that told stories about her culture—stories about animals and nature, the changing seasons, and the strength of her people. Other times, she kicked up her heels in the Charleston, a fast-paced American dance in which you swing your arms and twist your feet. She was so talented that she could move between old and new styles with ease.

At fifteen, she left home to join a traveling show. She danced under the name Molly Spotted Elk and learned new styles along the way. But some audiences didn't want real Native dances. They wanted a made-up version—with feathered headdresses and silly costumes that didn't reflect her heritage.

It made her sad to pretend to be someone she wasn't. But she knew the money she was earning was helping her family. She danced in Wild West shows, at rodeos, and in big cities like New York. Eventually, she starred in a silent movie called *The Silent Enemy* that told the story of a Native community from a long time ago. No stereotypes. No made-up nonsense. Just the truth—and Molly helped make sure of it.

It made her want to fulfill her biggest dream: to teach others about Penobscot culture in a meaningful, honest way. Not just in nightclubs. Not in costumes that weren't authentic. She wanted to be taken seriously—as an artist and a storyteller.

She found an opportunity in 1931, when she traveled to Paris, France, to perform with a Native dance troupe. She expected the usual—people laughing, mocking, not listening. But the crowds in Paris surprised her.

They were curious. They were respectful. They were eager to learn.

So when the show ended and the other dancers left France, Molly took a chance: She stayed.

"Maybe I am foolish, with no money, but hopes galore," she wrote in her diary. "But I DO want to do something with my Indian dancing here in a serious artistic way."

She gave lectures in museums. She danced in elegant halls. She wrote newspaper tales. She fell in love with a French journalist named Jean Archambaud, and they had a daughter.

In 1939, a publisher agreed to print her book of Penobscot stories—legends she had carefully written down. At the time, most Native stories were only passed down out loud. But Molly believed they deserved to be printed for the world to see.

Then World War II began. France went to battle. Her book deal vanished. Molly and her daughter escaped across the mountains into Spain when Germany invaded France. It was a long journey, mostly on foot. The plan was to reunite with Molly's husband. But she later learned that he had died.

The news broke her heart. She returned to Maine, where she spent a year recovering in a hospital.

But she didn't give up.

She made baskets and dolls. She taught children. And she kept telling Penobscot stories—the ones she had loved since she was a girl.

She died in 1977, at age seventy-three. But more than thirty years later, her book was finally published. It included a dictionary, translations, and her own voice—strong and clear.

Molly Nelson in 1928 wearing a floor-length feathered headdress, an example of the outfits she was made to wear to match audiences' stereotypes of Native Americans.

"To hear [the stories] in her words," a Penobscot friend said, "is to hear them in her elders' words."

Her stories still dance across the page, keeping Penobscot traditions alive.

TERRI ROGERS

A WOMAN OF MANY VOICES

A woman wearing a sparkly crown and a bright blue dress walks onto a stage holding a microphone in one hand. In the other is a doll—one that looks like a small man.

The woman starts talking to the audience, smiling wide.

But then a grumpy voice cuts her off to complain. It's the doll! It's talking!

"Do you mind?" she asks, turning to look at him.

"What's the matter now?" he whines.

"I'm trying to talk to the ladies and gentlemen," she says politely.

"Go ahead, go ahead, I'm not stopping you," he insists, then under his breath, he adds: "Silly old cow."

The audience bursts into laughter.

The woman's name is Terri Rogers, and the doll is called Shorty. They argue, laugh, and tell jokes—but there's a secret. Terri is doing both voices! When Shorty talks, Terri doesn't even move her lips. It's like magic.

That's called ventriloquism—making a puppet or doll seem like it's alive, with its own voice and personality. Shorty's eyebrows wiggled, his eyes blinked, and his mouth moved like he was thinking for himself. But Terri was controlling all his actions, using hidden dials and switches in his back.

"Ventriloquism comes from lip control, puppetry, and acting," the historian and ventriloquist Geoff Felix explained. "Many ventriloquists have two of these. Terri Rogers had all three."

Terri was born on May 4, 1937, in Ipswich, England. As a kid, she often felt lonely.

"Nobody would speak to me," she said, adding, "I wanted to prove that I was as good as, if not better than, anybody else."

She was around fifteen when she started studying her craft, after finding a little book about ventriloquism at a store. She bought it, took it home, and taught herself everything.

Terri Rogers around the 1960s with her doll, Shorty Harris. Together, they argued, laughed, and told jokes.

> **"I WANTED TO PROVE THAT I WAS AS GOOD AS, IF NOT BETTER THAN, ANYBODY ELSE."**

She started performing at nearby comedy theaters. When people saw how talented and funny she was, they invited her to be on TV. Soon she was on stages all over the world—in Las Vegas, Hollywood, even Bulgaria.

No matter where she was, or whether she was in front of huge crowds or television cameras, Terri never seemed nervous. She stood tall, kept calm, and sounded crisp, every word timed just right.

Her performance was even more extraordinary because Terri had another secret: She was transgender—born with a boy's body even though she knew she was a girl. Back then, it was hard for people like Terri to be accepted, so she kept that part of her life private. But onstage, none of that mattered. With her puppets and characters, she was able to express herself through her creativity and humor. Interestingly, Shorty was originally a girl puppet, until Terri gave him a new voice and personality.

Terri lived with her partner, Val Andrews, a magician who loved her very much. She cared deeply about her fans, and when she got sick and had to use a wheelchair, she kept traveling to meet them with Val's help.

Terri's voice and magic live on. You can still find videos of her and Shorty online—just one woman, one puppet, and a whole lot of talent.

Terri Rogers and Shorty Harris on *The Wheeltappers and Shunters Social Club,* in 1975.

Regina Jonas in 1936, a year after she was officially ordained as the world's first woman rabbi.

REGINA JONAS

THE FIRST WOMAN RABBI

Regina Sara Jonas was born on August 3, 1902, in Germany.

She grew up in the bustling city of Berlin, where the streets echoed with footsteps and prayer songs. At home and in synagogue, she listened as rabbis taught about Jewish life. But there was one thing she couldn't help noticing: Every rabbi was a man.

Regina wanted to change that. She loved her faith deeply. She studied its teachings with joy and care. And she believed that girls should have the chance to lead, too.

God didn't care about gender, she said. "Therefore, it is the duty of men and women alike to work and create according to the skills given by God."

As a young woman, she sat down to write a bold essay. The topic: Can women be rabbis? Her answer wasn't just yes. She decided she would *become* a rabbi.

But the path wasn't easy. She knocked on doors, asked questions, studied harder than ever. And when she asked her teacher to be ordained—to be officially made a rabbi—his answer was no.

Finally, in 1935, one brave rabbi said yes. He saw what others had missed: Regina's fierce mind, steady heart, and deep love for her community. When she was ordained, she made history. She was the first woman to ever be ordained as a rabbi.

"We really cannot help but stand in awe of her courage," said Sally Priesand, the second woman to be ordained as a rabbi, nearly forty years later. "All female rabbis stand on her shoulders."

But synagogues wouldn't hire Regina. So she went where she was needed most—hospitals, nursing homes, prisons. She sat by people's bedsides. She prayed with the sick. She listened to the lonely. Her voice was soft but strong. She reminded people that they mattered.

When World War II began and the Nazis started attacking Jewish communities, many rabbis fled. Regina said she could not abandon anyone who was suffering.

Later, she was sent to a concentration camp—a brutal prison for Jewish people and others whom the Nazis wanted to harm. Even there, she continued being a rabbi. She led prayers. She offered comfort. She kept hope alive.

"What I find most extraordinary about her," said the scholar Katharina von Kellenbach, "is that she decided to deny the Nazis the power to define Jewish life."

Today, women make up more than half the students in many rabbinical schools in the United States and England. Some lead the biggest synagogues in the world. Many of them thank Regina for paving the way. They even idolize her.

But for Regina, it wasn't about fame. She was just following her true calling.

"For me it was never about being the first," she said. "I wish I had been the hundred thousandth!"

Berlin's Neue Synagogue, in 1900.

THE RABBI WHO BROKE BARRIERS IN AMERICA

Just like Regina Jonas had in Germany, Sally J. Priesand made history—but this time in the United States. When she was twenty-five, she became the first woman officially ordained as a rabbi in America—meaning she was formally recognized as a Jewish religious leader.

She had decided she wanted to be a rabbi when she was sixteen. When she asked the teachers at her Jewish school about it, they said no. "We do not know what opportunities exist for women," they said. That didn't stop her, and she was ordained in 1972.

Even so, no synagogue would hire her. Finally, in 1981, she became the rabbi at Monmouth Reform Temple in Tinton Falls, New Jersey. It was the home she had been searching for. She led holy services, taught Hebrew school, comforted people who were sick, and performed weddings and funerals.

Her courage opened doors for thousands of women, showing that faith, leadership, and big dreams aren't limited by gender.

LORENZA BÖTTNER

PAINTING WITHOUT LIMITS

When Lorenza Böttner was around nine years old, she had a really bad accident.

She was on her way to school when she saw feathers drifting down from the sky. She looked up and saw an electrical tower. There must have been birds on top! Maybe even a whole nest of them. Lorenza loved animals—*especially* birds. How nice would it be to have a baby bird as a pet? Lorenza was climbing up the tower to investigate when the mother bird suddenly flapped her wings. It startled Lorenza, and she lost her balance. Quickly, to stop herself from falling, she reached for the nearest thing: a live electrical wire.

Both of her arms were badly burned. Lorenza's mother rushed her to the hospital, where doctors said they would have to remove Lorenza's arms.

No arms?! How could Lorenza live with no arms? She *needed* her arms—to play with toys, to draw pictures, to wave them in the air as she danced around her bedroom.

Lorenza wanted to hide. But her mother told her not to give up and sent her to a special school where she could learn alongside other children with disabilities. She gave her a pencil, and Lorenza learned to write with her mouth and her feet. As she grew older, Lorenza did *everything* with her mouth and her feet.

She got ready in the morning by pulling her dress over her head using her teeth. She cooked dinner by lifting the pot with her toes. She painted by putting a brush between her lips.

Lorenza was in control of her life again.

When she grew up, she attended college, where she studied art, and then she became an artist and a dancer. Sometimes she would make art and dance *at the same time*. She put on music, spread a giant sheet of paper on the floor, and danced across it, painting with her feet as she went.

She did this on the sidewalks and in plazas and onstage. She didn't want pity. She wanted people to see the power and joy she felt in being different.

Lorenza Böttner in 1984 at New York University, where she studied. She often had clothing custom made for her body.

Lorenza Böttner in 1983. After she lost her arms in a childhood accident, her mother encouraged her to create art with her mouth and her feet.

“THROUGH ART, LORENZA COULD EXPRESS HERSELF . . .”

And people weren’t just amazed by what she was able to *do;* they were amazed by her *talent*—lively brushstrokes full of movement, color, and feeling.

Lorenza was born on March 6, 1959, in Punta Arenas, Chile. She was told she was a boy, but deep down she knew she was a girl. She wore dresses and makeup and grew her hair long. Her mother was very supportive. She believed that Lorenza should be whomever she truly was inside.

Through art, Lorenza could express herself—her identity, her gender, her disability, her beauty. She painted many versions of herself: a woman with long hair, a man in a suit, and someone with no arms. She believed that people were layered and complex, and that one person could be many things at the same time.

Often, she painted herself with wings. “Birds have always fascinated me,” she once said, “their lightness and the freedom to fly away and go wherever they please.”

Lorenza’s art lives on today. Her work has been shown in museums around the world, proving to people that beauty means learning to soar—in your own unique way.

Ruby Payne-Scott in an undated photograph. In the 1940s, she helped lay the foundation for a new field of science called radio astronomy.

RUBY PAYNE-SCOTT

THE WOMAN WHO HEARD THE SUN

The sun doesn't talk. It doesn't scream or whisper. But it *does* make noises—through strange, invisible waves that ripple across space like silent music.

Ruby Payne-Scott was one of the first people in history to hear the sun. Not with her ears, but with a machine called a radio telescope. The sounds—which reminded her of popcorn kernels bursting in a pan, the hum of a crackling campfire, or the *whoosh* of a sudden gust of wind—surprised her.

Ruby was born on May 28, 1912, in Grafton, New South Wales, Australia. Back then, it was very rare for girls—especially from small towns like hers—to go to college. Most girls were expected to focus on home and family, not science or school. But Ruby was curious and clever, asking questions like: Why does the moon change shape? What makes a ball bounce? What is lightning made of?

Because she studied hard in school, Ruby got the chance to go to college, where she studied physics—the science of how things move, work, and connect—and began learning the answers to some of her questions.

After college, Ruby became a schoolteacher and then took a job where she fixed radios. When World War II began, the government needed smart people like Ruby to work on top-secret projects to keep the country safe. She worked in a lab, using radio waves to listen for Japanese airplanes before they could attack. But some of the signals sounded different—bursts of noise that weren't coming from planes at all. They were coming from the sun.

At the time, no one knew that the sun could send out radio waves. Ruby helped prove that it could. And some of those waves are so powerful that they can affect electronics on Earth.

Her discovery led to a new type of science called radio astronomy—a way of listening to space instead of just looking at it. She opened a new window into the universe that uncovered mysteries like exploding stars and black holes.

No one had been to space yet, but when Ruby tuned in to the sky's strange signals, it felt like traveling. Like freedom.

Back on Earth, life wasn't so free. Ruby had gotten married while she was working in the secret lab, which was a problem because women who worked for the government in Australia were expected to quit their jobs if they got married. Ruby loved her job *and* her husband. Why did she have to choose? Her friends agreed that she didn't. They would help keep her marriage a secret. She even wore her wedding ring on a chain around her neck so no one could see it—a quiet act of rebellion. Had she left her job, she never would have made her big discovery about the sun.

Eventually, the secret got out. Ruby was forced to leave her job. She started speaking up—for women, for fairness, for the right to choose your own path. After a while, she got her job back, but she didn't stay long, excited to become a mother instead.

Ruby didn't just change how we understand the universe. She helped people see that women belong in science—and anywhere else they want to be.

Ruby Payne-Scott in 1952 at the International Union of Radio Science conference at the University of Sydney.

FROM THE SUN TO THE MOON

Ruby Payne-Scott used science to help people study the sun. Judith Love Cohen, on the other hand, helped them study the moon.

In the 1960s, the U.S. government had a new idea: to send astronauts to the moon—a place no human had ever visited. What was it like there? Astronauts wanted to explore, to learn, to do the impossible. The government called this mission the Apollo program.

Judith was an engineer who worked on the program and created something called the Abort Guidance System. It was meant to help astronauts if they were in trouble—which is exactly what happened in 1970. When an oxygen tank on a space rocket exploded, the system helped guide the astronauts back to Earth, saving their lives.

Judith's work didn't stop there. She contributed to the Hubble Space Telescope, which allows us to see distant galaxies and stars in amazing detail. And she wrote a series of children's books about women in science, starting with *You Can Be a Woman Engineer.* "By the time she was done," her son Neil Siegel said, "she must have influenced tens of thousands of girls."

ROLAND JOHNSON

WHOSE VOICE MADE US LISTEN

Roland Johnson was born on September 14, 1945, in Philadelphia, Pennsylvania. His parents had nine children and worked very hard to support them. Roland was neurodiverse, which means he thought differently than most people, and he sometimes needed extra help understanding things.

No school would take Roland, so his parents kept him at home. They tried their best to watch him, but Roland often got into trouble—running away or stealing food from stores.

Eventually, his parents asked the government for help. Roland was sent to a special school called Pennhurst, where there were other students with disabilities.

But it wasn't really a school. It felt more like a prison.

"This is it for me," he remembered thinking. "I guess I will be locked up in there, in a big cellar with locks."

The building was cold. The air smelled like bleach and old clothes. Doors slammed shut with a loud clang. At night, Roland hid under his bed, pressing his body against the wall, trying not to cry. He heard screaming down the hall. He held his breath when the staff walked by, afraid they'd notice him.

The people working there were cruel. They called him "stupid" and "dummy." He saw other kids get hurt—pushed and slapped. When they cried, the staff ignored them.

During the day, he was forced to work—cleaning floors, doing laundry, and even taking care of younger children. "Nobody got paid," he wrote. "They would work, work, work."

Roland stayed there for thirteen terrible years. He felt lost and lonely, like he was "in a desert world."

Then something changed. In 1968, a TV reporter showed the world what was really happening at Pennhurst. People were shocked. The documentary was called *Suffer the Little Children*. Pennhurst was soon called "the shame of the nation."

Roland Johnson (1945–1994) escaped mistreatment at an institution and became an activist for people with disabilities.

Roland Johnson spoke out on behalf of people with disabilities and successfully argued that they should be able to live independently.

Thanks to that report—and to people like Roland, who talked about what he had been through—Pennhurst was shut down.

Roland moved back home. Things were still hard. He had trouble getting along with his family. He struggled with his health. But with time, and the right support, he started to heal.

He got a job as a janitor. He found his own apartment. For the first time, he had a key that was his. He could lock the door when he wanted. He could decorate the walls. He could make his own breakfast and sit in quiet, without anyone shouting.

And most important, he found his voice. He started speaking out for other people with disabilities. He gave speeches. He went to courtrooms. He stood on stages and asked: "Who's in control?"

» THE LAW THAT HELPED EVERYONE BELONG

The Americans with Disabilities Act (ADA) is a law that was passed in 1990. It makes sure that people with disabilities have the same rights and opportunities as everyone else. That means no one can be left out at work, at school, or in public places just because of a disability.

The ADA led to changes you probably see every day:

- Ramps and elevators so wheelchairs can reach every floor
- Curb cuts, which were built at first for people in wheelchairs but have also made it easier for strollers, bikes, and scooters to roll smoothly from the sidewalk to the street
- Braille signs so people who are blind can read important information
- Closed captions so people who are deaf or hard of hearing can follow TV shows and movies
- Service animals—like dogs trained to help people with disabilities—being allowed in restaurants and stores and on buses and trains
- Accessible transportation—buses, trains, and subways with ramps, lifts, or spaces for wheelchairs so everyone can get around

These changes don't just help people with disabilities—they make life easier for everyone. That's why the ADA is one of the most important civil rights laws in U.S. history.

"ROLAND GAVE VOICE TO THE PEOPLE..."

His answer: "You are."

Because of his work, more people with disabilities were able to live independently, not locked up in hospitals. They got jobs, went to school, and had more control over their lives. He also helped shut down other schools like Pennhurst.

When the Americans with Disabilities Act—a new law protecting the rights of people with disabilities—was signed by President George H. W. Bush at the White House in 1990, Roland was there. The sun was bright. The crowd clapped and cheered. Roland stood tall. He later offered an award to the president for his work to end discrimination against people with disabilities.

"Roland gave voice to the people," one leader said. "Roland made us listen."

He changed how we think about disability. And he helped change the world. Change that lasts to this day.

Roland Johnson in 1993 presenting an award to President George H.W. Bush for his work to ban discrimination against people with disabilities.

Usha Mehta with a cutout of Mahatma Gandhi in Mumbai in 1997. She gave daily radio news bulletins during Gandhi's Quit India campaign, until she was arrested.

USHA MEHTA

A VOICE OF FREEDOM

Usha (pronounced OO-sha) Mehta sat alone in a dark basement. The windows were covered. The lights were off. Only the glow of a single lantern lit the desk in front of her.

She leaned forward and began to speak into a microphone.

Then—

BANG! BANG! BANG!

Fists pounded on the door.

Usha froze. Her mouth went dry. She knew what would happen if she was caught. She also knew she couldn't stop now. She took a breath and kept speaking.

The door burst open. Fifty police officers barged in, grabbed her, and forced her into their van. She was going to jail.

What had she done wrong? She had told the truth. And that was a problem.

This was in 1942 in India, when the British rulers of the country mistreated Indians and punished anyone who complained. The British controlled the newspapers, so Usha found another way to spread the truth: by radio.

It was dangerous. It was bold. And it was exactly what she felt she had to do.

But she hadn't always been a rule breaker.

Usha was born in a small village named Saras on March 25, 1920. When she was older, her family moved to Bombay—a big city in India now called Mumbai—where she sat quietly in class, did her chores, and completed her homework.

But there was one rule she could never accept: that her country belonged to another country.

Before Usha was even born, India had been taken over by the British. They controlled the government, the money, and the laws, but they weren't interested in helping Indian people.

Rather, most of their decisions *hurt* Indian people. Farmers were forced to grow crops that the British wanted, not food for their own families. Factories sent goods back to Britain instead of to local markets. Indian workers were paid less than British ones, and Indian children had fewer chances to go to school. Many people became poor.

Basically, the British acted like they were better than Indians—just because of the color of their skin.

Then came Mahatma Gandhi. Gandhi was a leader with vision—not just for India, but for the world. Gandhi believed that people could fight for change without violence. He believed that Indians deserved the right to make their own choices and build a better future, and he asked people like Usha to help make it happen.

Usha was in school, studying law, when she left to help Gandhi. She and her friends created Congress Radio—a station that transmitted messages across the country. As Gandhi organized protests, Usha told listeners where they were happening. She told true stories of everyday people who stood up to injustice and succeeded. Her messages motivated more and more people to get involved.

Every broadcast came with a risk because the police were looking for Usha and her friends. They moved constantly, carrying their equipment in bags, whispering code words, never staying in one place for long.

"This is Congress Radio, calling on 42.34 meters, from somewhere in India," Usha would say each time.

Eventually, the police tracked them down. One morning, while Usha was on the air, they surrounded the building. She told the others to escape. Then she stayed, still broadcasting, until the police broke down the door.

She spent nearly four years in prison—much of it in solitary confinement.

In 1947, a year after she was finally released, India gained its independence. Soon after, it passed its first constitution, which said that people have the right to freedom of speech and expression.

Thanks to Usha's voice, India found its own.

> **SHE TOLD TRUE STORIES OF EVERYDAY PEOPLE WHO STOOD UP TO INJUSTICE.**

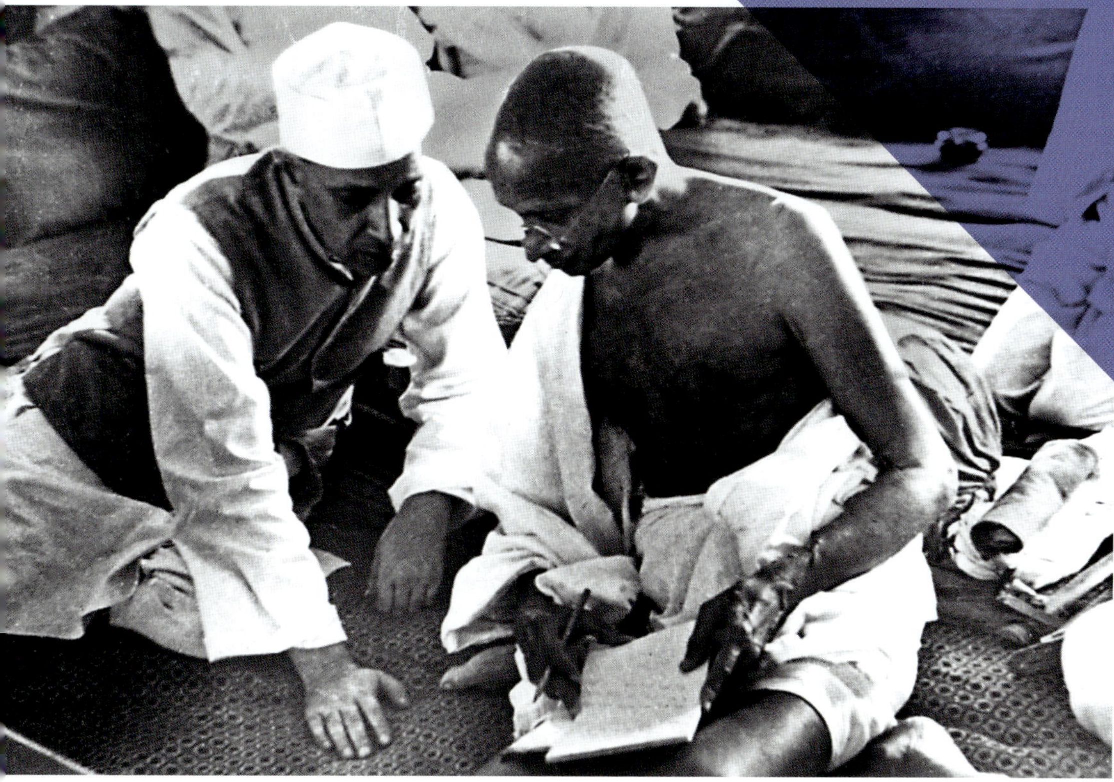

Mahatma Gandhi and Pandit J. Nehru during the All India Congress Committee Session, 1942, when the Quit India Resolution was adopted. Nehru became India's first prime minister.

ANDRA 1927 BUILDIN
HANI BOO OT

A procession of freedom fighters in Bombay during the Quit India movement started by Gandhi.

MIKI GORMAN

WHO FOUND COURAGE ONE MILE AT A TIME

Miki Gorman sat in a restaurant eating two giant crepes stuffed with mushrooms, spinach, and eggs. A couple sitting nearby couldn't stop staring: Miki was a small woman, yet she was devouring so much food.

Miki noticed the stares and smiled. "I'm running the New York City Marathon tomorrow," she told the couple. "And I'm going to win!"

They looked surprised. But the next day, Miki did exactly what she'd said she would: She crossed the finish line before any other woman. Then she came back the next year and won *again*. After that, no American woman would win the New York City Marathon for another *forty years*.

Miki's journey wasn't easy, though.

She was born on August 9, 1935, in Qingdao, China. Her parents were from Japan, and she helped take care of her two younger brothers. Her family didn't have much money. Some days, the only food they had was a small bowl of rice and some soybeans. The cupboards were otherwise empty.

"We all looked like skeletons," Miki said later. "We were always hungry."

Her father was strict. She wanted to be a violinist, but he wanted her to focus on school. And whenever he gave her a gift, he insisted that she untangle the strings on the package instead of just ripping it open.

"These [lessons from my dad] seem meaningless, but actually taught me a lot—discipline, patience, and to never give up," she later said. "I think that mental discipline had a lot to do with my running."

When she grew up, she moved to the United States, where she worked as a nanny and as a secretary in an office. She also got married and had a daughter.

One day, she confided in her husband about something that had bothered her for a long time: her size. At about five feet tall and only 90 pounds, she was so much

Miki Gorman in 1974, the year she won the Boston Marathon. She is the only woman known to have won the New York City and Boston Marathons twice.

smaller than most American women, who were on average several inches taller and closer to 140 pounds. She also spoke with a soft voice. People thought of her as fragile, and that made her feel invisible—like they only thought of her as half a person.

Her husband suggested they go for a run. It might build her strength, he told her, and perhaps she would even eat more. He didn't know that it would also reveal her superpower. Miki was *fast,* and she could go for very long distances without getting tired. Soon she started running races and winning trophies. Then she set her sights on one of the most challenging races in the world: the New York City Marathon.

A marathon is long—26.2 miles. For some people, that's like running from morning until dinner without stopping.

Miki Gorman, winner of the 1976 New York City Marathon.

“BEING SMALL DIDN’T MEAN BEING WEAK...”

To get ready, Miki trained for hours each day. She ran up hills. She pushed through pain. There were days she didn’t want to run. Days when her legs ached and the rain beat down on her face. But she got up and did it, again and again.

On the day of the marathon, the wind blew hard and cold. Miki tucked behind taller runners so she wouldn’t be pushed back. Her feet hurt from running over a metal bridge. And at one point, a giant dog ran up and tried to lick her!

But Miki didn’t give up. With the finish line ahead, she used every bit of strength she had left. She passed the runners in front of her, one by one. The crowds were screaming, “First woman! First woman!” It lifted Miki’s spirits and made her run even faster.

“I’ll never forget that feeling,” she said.

When she crossed the finish line first, she felt proud. Her heart raced. She had done it. All the doubts—about her size, her abilities, her worth—melted away.

And guess who was at the finish line? The couple from the night before at the restaurant. They were shocked—and impressed. The tiny woman who’d eaten two giant crepes had really won the women’s race.

She proved to them that strength doesn’t always look the way people expect it to—that being small didn’t mean being weak. And now the whole world knew, too.

Gladys Bentley, performing in her top hat and tuxedo, became 1920s-era Harlem royalty.

GLADYS BENTLEY

WHO GLOWED UNDER THE HARLEM LIGHTS

About a hundred years ago, a neighborhood in New York City called Harlem came alive with music, art, dancing, and poetry. This exciting time was called the Harlem Renaissance.

Black artists were showing the world their talents—and their pride. They were saying: We matter. Our stories matter. Our thoughts matter. And one voice rang out louder than most: that of the bold singer Gladys Bentley.

Gladys was a piano player who wrote her own songs, which she performed in Harlem nightclubs in the 1920s and '30s. Inside those clubs, the warm air smelled like sweet cigar smoke and spicy food. People crowded around tiny tables, fanning themselves with folded napkins, their faces glowing under the soft yellow light. Glasses clinked. Laughter echoed. The piano sparkled as it waited for Gladys to sit down, straighten her tuxedo, and place her fingers on the keys.

Then—boom!—her voice filled the room. It was loud and low and full of joy. She sang with a wink, a growl, a giggle. She made up silly, sassy lyrics on the spot. Her hands danced across the piano like they had minds of their own.

The crowd loved her. People clapped, stomped their feet, and sang along. Sometimes she strutted through the room, smiling, teasing, flirting with women in the front row.

Gladys was a lesbian, and she didn't hide it. That made her very brave. Back then, people could get into trouble just for being themselves. But Gladys kept showing up, singing loud, and dressing the way she liked—often in men's clothing, including a tall white top hat.

One famous poet, Langston Hughes, called her "an amazing exhibition of musical energy—a large, dark, masculine lady, whose feet pounded the floor while her fingers pounded the keyboard—a perfect piece of African sculpture, animated by her own rhythm."

"WE MATTER. OUR STORIES MATTER. OUR THOUGHTS MATTER."

Gladys was born on August 12, 1907, and grew up in Philadelphia, Pennsylvania. She usually had crushes on other girls, rather than on boys. Her parents did not understand her feelings, and she often felt lonely. But she found comfort in music. She taught herself to play the piano and began writing songs.

At just sixteen years old, Gladys left home and moved to New York City. Harlem was bursting with life. There were house parties, dance halls, and hidden clubs where people gathered.

Gladys became a star. People came from all over to see her perform. She lived in a fancy apartment and had a driver and servants. But she was most famous for being bold—singing about love, heartbreak, and what it meant to live proudly as herself.

When people told her to quiet down, Gladys sang louder. She showed the world what it meant to be free.

Blues singer and pianist Gladys Bentley poses for a portrait circa 1930 in New York City.

ÁNGELA RUIZ ROBLES

INVENTOR OF THE AMAZING BOOK MACHINE

Every school day, when Ángela Ruiz Robles saw her students struggling under the weight of their heavy backpacks, she thought, So many books! Their poor little backs!

Ángela was born on March 28, 1895, in Villamanín, a small town in Spain. She grew up to become a teacher, a mother of three, and a big believer in learning. She wanted to make life easier for her students—and for kids everywhere.

So she sat down and imagined something new: a machine that could hold all the books a kid might need. On any subject. In any language. All in one place.

She called it the Mechanical Encyclopedia.

It looked like a pale green lunch box about the size of a textbook, but it weighed less, and inside, it was packed with clever ideas. There were scrolls you could swap in and out depending on what you wanted to read. It had a lightbulb so it could be used in the dark, a magnifying glass to help students see tiny letters, and even a calculator to do math. And it ran on batteries! This all-in-one device was designed to make learning easier and more fun.

Ángela's invention was basically an e-reader—kind of like a Kindle or an iPad—but she built it more than sixty years before those existed. And she didn't work for a big company like Apple or Amazon. She did it all by herself, at home.

"What she invented carried on into the future," her grandson Daniel said, adding, "Each time I see an e-reader, I am reminded of my grandmother."

To show how it worked, she built a prototype—that means a test version of an invention. She even got a patent, which is an official way of saying, *This idea is mine, and no one else can copy it without permission.*

Daniel said she worked nonstop.

"She never wasted time," he said. "She didn't look at the birds. She was always working."

Ángela Ruiz Robles with some of her Mechanical Encylopedias, which was a pale green box about the size of a textbook that allowed a user to read any book in any language and on any topic.

Ángela presenting her invention to the mayor of Ferrol, Spain.

> **WHAT SHE INVENTED CARRIED ON INTO THE FUTURE.**

Ángela tried for years to get factories to make copies of her Mechanical Encyclopedia. She wanted kids all over the world to use it. But no one said yes. So she used the only one she made to teach students in her classroom, and she shared it with her own children as well.

Even though her invention never made it to store shelves, Ángela's big idea didn't disappear. Today, you can see her prototype in a science museum in Spain. And every time someone picks up an e-reader, in a way, they're holding a little piece of her dream.

Emily Warren Roebling in 1899. She led the project to build the Brooklyn Bridge after her husband, the engineer, became ill.

EMILY WARREN ROEBLING

THE WOMAN WHO BRIDGED A CITY

There is a saying: Behind every great man is a great woman.

Emily Warren Roebling was that great woman. And the great man was her husband, Washington A. Roebling.

Washington was an engineer who was responsible for supervising the construction of the Brooklyn Bridge in New York City. The bridge, which had been designed by Washington's father, John A. Roebling, would connect Manhattan with Brooklyn, and it would be the longest bridge of its kind in the world when it was completed in 1883.

But just a couple of years into the bridge's construction, Washington got sick. *Really* sick. At the time, doctors didn't know what was happening—many workers who went deep underground got sick in the same way. Now we know that it was a disease called decompression sickness, also known as the bends. It was so serious that he couldn't leave his bed. Some days, he couldn't even see or speak. He was supposed to be the chief engineer of the Brooklyn Bridge, but now he couldn't set foot on the construction site.

As it turned out, Emily had learned a lot about engineering from working alongside her husband. But none of the workers believed she could help build the bridge because she was a woman. At first, she passed along her husband's instructions. She became his "eyes and ears," as one person put it.

But soon people realized she had ideas of her own, and she started doing much more than just passing along messages. She met with city officials and helped solve problems that came up during construction. She made decisions about materials and deadlines. She even suggested design improvements that made parts of the bridge stronger and more efficient. She wasn't just helping—she was leading the project.

Emily was born on September 23, 1843, in Cold Spring, New York, and had eleven brothers and sisters. She loved learning subjects like history, astronomy, and algebra—things most girls weren't encouraged to study back then. Her husband admired her intelligence, which wasn't something men usually noticed about women in those days.

After Washington became sick, Emily tied on her bonnet and went to the noisy construction site each morning. If Washington felt strong enough, he would watch her through a telescope from his bedroom.

She walked past workers shouting to each other, clouds of dust, and the sounds of hammers banging against steel. The East River shimmered below, and the towers of the bridge's frame loomed like stone giants.

> **"SHE WASN'T JUST HELPING—SHE WAS LEADING..."**

"I don't think that the Brooklyn Bridge would be standing were it not for her," said Erica Wagner, who wrote a book about Washington.

It took fourteen years and several thousand workers to build the bridge. When it was finally done, it was called the "eighth wonder of the world." There was even a fireworks show to celebrate. Emily was the first person to walk across the bridge. She brought a rooster with her for good luck.

Today there is a plaque on the bridge that honors the Roebling family. It says: "Back of every great work we can find the self-sacrificing devotion of a woman." That sounds old-fashioned now, but it was meant to recognize Emily's work at a time when women weren't expected to do important things outside the home. Emily didn't just support her family—she helped build one of the most famous bridges in the world.

Each day, thousands of people cross the Brooklyn Bridge—just like Emily once did when she took that proud first step with her rooster, the whole city watching.

The bridge opened on May 24, 1883, connecting Manhattan and Brooklyn.

ROSE MACKENBERG

SHE DIDN'T CHASE GHOSTS. SHE CHASED THE TRUTH.

A woman sat at a table in flickering candlelight. A curtain rustled. Somewhere, a bell rang.

"Your mother is with us," she whispered.

On the other side of the table, Harry Houdini felt his skin tingle with anticipation.

Harry was a magician who could escape from locked trunks, jail cells, and handcuffs. But there was one thing he couldn't escape: heartbreak.

When his beloved mother died in 1913, people told Harry they could help him speak with her again. They called themselves mediums and said they could talk to the dead. Oh, how desperate Harry was to talk to his mother. Was it really possible?

To find out, he sometimes agreed to see these mediums at séances—meetings where people tried to contact ghosts.

The rooms were often thick with candle smoke. The tables would wobble mysteriously, and objects would float in the air.

But one of the mediums made a mistake. She scribbled down a message for Harry from his mother—in English. Harry's mother didn't speak English. She spoke Hungarian, German, and Yiddish. But not English.

The medium was lying, and that made Harry furious. Not just for himself but for all the people with broken hearts who were being duped. These mediums weren't just performing magic tricks. They were taking advantage of people's grief. And Harry wanted to stop them.

There were a lot of mediums out there. Harry knew he couldn't catch all of them alone, so he hired twenty people to help him. Their leader was Rose Mackenberg, a private detective who had been born on July 10, 1892, in Brooklyn, New York. Rose had started out working in a law office, where she took notes and prepared papers for the lawyers. But she was so smart, sharp, and skeptical that people started asking her to investigate cases on the side—and she could spot a lie from a mile away.

Rose Mackenberg in 1945. In a career that lasted decades, she attended hundreds of séances to expose fake psychics.

Rose didn't chase ghosts. She chased the truth.

She didn't look like a typical detective—especially not in 1920s America when detectives were mostly men—but that only helped her.

powers. It is not my intention to criticize them now or hereafter, and nothing that I shall write should be construed as reflecting on their characters.

But to get back to Houdini's alleged spirit message to his widow, Beatrice. The first intimation that Harry had actually "got through" a

that she was ill. She had fallen fainting in her home on New Year's Day, and as she talked her dark, queenly head was swathed in bandages.

Mrs. Balbina Rahner, Mrs. Houdini's mother

Mrs. Houdini had no recollection of c
but a few nights later she had dreamed t
appeared to her, saying, "Thank God,
(a nickname), at last you have found

The Author of This Revelation

How Miss M

As a Smartly Garbed Widow.

As a Rustic Schoolteacher.

As a Small Town Matron.

As a Credulous Servant

She wore costumes to hundreds of séances. Sometimes she wore a black veil. Sometimes she brought a cane and pretended to limp. She played the part of a grieving widow or mother. The mediums always believed her. And they claimed to hear the voices of her loved ones—even when Rose had made them up.

Some of the many disguises Rose Mackenberg wore to séances, as depicted in a 1929 newspaper article. With each character, she employed pseudonyms such as "Allicia Bunck" (or "all is a bunk") and Frances Raud ("F. Raud" or "fraud").

Rose Mackenberg uncovered so many fake mediums that a lot of people stopped going to them.

"YOU CAN LEARN THE TRUTH BY ASKING THE RIGHT QUESTIONS..."

Rose exposed more than a thousand frauds. She used fake names—or pseudonyms—like Frances Raud or F. Raud. (Get it? Fraud.)

"I never married," she told a reporter, "but I have received messages from 1,000 husbands and twice as many children in the world to come. Invariably they told me they were happy where they were, which was not entirely flattering to me."

Rose gave lectures on how to spot a phony medium and revealed their tricks, like using a hidden harmonica to create ghostly noises.

Rose and Harry went to the government to ask them to ban mediums. The government ultimately said no, but by this point Harry and Rose had uncovered so many fake mediums that a lot of people stopped going to them anyway.

Deep down, though, Rose always wondered if ghosts were real. She said she slept with the lights on at home—just to be safe.

Rose proved you don't have to believe everything you're told. You can learn the truth by asking the right questions, even if the truth is harder to hear.

HOW TO WRITE AN OBITUARY

An obituary is a story about someone who has died. It usually includes basic facts: when and where they were born, who their family members were, where they lived, and what they did for work or for fun.

But an obituary isn't *just* a list of facts. It's about showing what made that person unique. Did they love to sing? Tell great jokes? Work hard to help their community? What did people admire about them? Those details bring the story to life.

When journalists write obituaries, they gather information from many places. They interview family and friends. They read letters or journals that the person wrote. They look at photos, social media, and records like birth certificates. Then they choose the most important parts that capture the person's story.

Try it yourself.

Pick someone you'd like to remember—a relative, a teacher, a neighbor, even a pet. Write a short obituary that includes a few facts and at least one detail that shows who they really were.

❶ Write down the basics.

- When and where they were born, if you can find out
- Who their family members were
- Where they may have lived, if they moved away from their birthplace

❷ Add personal details.

- What did they do, for work or for fun?
- What about them made people laugh or smile?
- Did they have any favorite sayings, foods, hobbies, or habits?

❸ Show their impact.

- How did this person (or pet) make a difference in other people's lives?
- Did they help their neighbors, create something new, or inspire others?

❹ Put it all together.

Start with the basic facts, then add the details that show the person's personality and what made them unique. Keep it short, clear, and heartfelt.

❺ Share and remember.

You can write this just for yourself, share it with family and friends, or even add a drawing or photograph. However you do it, you're helping to keep the person's memory alive.

Remember: Obituaries don't just tell us that someone existed. They help us remember how they lived their lives and how they made a difference for the people around them.

ACKNOWLEDGMENTS

This book wouldn't exist without the many talented writers and editors at *The New York Times* and beyond who have supported and contributed to the Overlooked series.

Thank you also to the librarians, archivists, and historians who do the hard work of excavating and preserving information that allows storytellers to bring these lives to light.

A huge thanks to my editor, my agent, and the publishing team for helping shape this adaptation for young readers.

And of course, thank you to my family, friends, mentors, and young test readers who encouraged curiosity, boldness, and asking big questions—you know who you are. Special thanks to Jodi and her son, Noah, for their incredible help.

Finally, to the remarkable people in this book: Your lives show that courage, creativity, and kindness can change the world.

PHOTOGRAPHY CREDITS

Gladys Bentley
page 74: Michael Ochs Archives/Getty Images
page 77: Edward Elcha/Michael Ochs Archives/Getty Images

Lorenza Böttner
page 51: Courtesy of Denise Katz Howick
page 52: Courtesy of Leslie-Lohman Museum of Art

Miki Gorman
page 71: Bettmann Archive/Getty Images
page 72: Aflo Co. Ltd./Alamy

Alison Hargreaves
page 17: PA Images via Getty Images

Roland Johnson
pages 59 and 60: Vision for Equality
page 63: AB Historic/Alamy

Regina Jonas
page 46: New Synagogue Berlin—Centrum Judaicum Foundation (CJ), Photo Archive
page 48: DHM/Kaiserpanorama/ullstein bild via Getty Images

Ralph Lazo
page 25: Japanese American National Museum, gift of Rose Hanawa Tanaka
page 26: Bettmann/Getty Images
page 29: Japanese American National Museum, gift of Rose Hanawa Tanaka

Rose Mackenberg
page 87: Special Collections Research Center/Temple University Libraries
pages 88 and 90: Public domain

Usha Mehta
page 64: Savita Kirloskar/Reuters
page 67: Bettmann/Getty Images
page 68: Dinodia Photos/Alamy

Molly Nelson
pages 38 and 41: Courtesy of Barbara Moore

Ruby Payne-Scott
pages 54 and 56: Australia Telescope National Facility

Qiu Jin
page 35: Public domain
page 36: Wisconsin Historical Society

Sarah E. Ray
page 30: Ronald Ernst/*Detroit News*

Ángela Ruiz Robles
pages 79 and 80: Courtesy of Ángela Ruiz Robles Family

Emily Warren Roebling
page 82: New-York Historical Society Library
page 85: Archivio GBB/Alamy

Terri Rogers
page 43: The Dezo Hoffmann Collection/Shutterstock
page 45: ITV/Shutterstock

Annie Edson Taylor
page 10: Pictorial Press Ltd/Alamy
page 12: M. H. Zahner/Library of Congress
page 15: Imago Images

Major Taylor
page 20: Library of Congress/Getty Images
page 23: NYPL/Interim Archives/Getty Images

Versions of many of the obituaries that appear in this volume were originally published in *The New York Times*. Inquiries concerning permissions to reprint any obituary (or portion thereof) which originally appeared in *The New York Times* newspaper should be addressed to The New York Times Company c/o Wright's Media at https://nytimes.wrightsmedia.com/.

TEN SPEED YOUNG READERS
An imprint of the Crown Publishing Group
A division of Penguin Random House LLC
1745 Broadway
New York, NY 10019
tenspeed.com
penguinrandomhouse.com

Photography credits are located on page 95.

Typefaces: J Foundry's Marsden, Mark Simonson Studio's Proxima Nova, ParaType's Simon, and Monotype's Rhetoric.

Library of Congress Cataloging-in-Publication Data is on file with the publisher.
Names: Padnani, Amisha author | New York Times Company issuing body
Title: The woman who heard the sun and other true stories overlooked by history / Amisha Padnani and the Obituaries Desk of The New York Times.
Description: First edition. | California : Ten Speed Young Readers, an imprint of Ten Speed Press, [2026] | Identifiers: LCCN 2026006596 (print) | LCCN 2026006597 (ebook) | ISBN 9780593837184 hardcover | ISBN 9780593837191 ebook
Subjects: LCSH: Biography | Obituaries | Heroes | Women | Minorities | LCGFT: Biographies
Classification: LCC CT107 .P235 2026 (print) | LCC CT107 (ebook) | DDC 920—dc23/eng/20260406
LC record available at https://lccn.loc.gov/2026006596
LC ebook record available at https://lccn.loc.gov/2026

Hardcover ISBN 978-0-593-83718-4
Ebook ISBN 978-0-593-83719-1

Editor: Ginee Seo | Production editor: Terry Deal | Assistant editor: Adah Li
Designer: Monica Cheng | Design manager: Kelly Booth | Production designer: Mari Gill
Production: Philip Leung | Photo retoucher: Claudia Sanchez
Copy editor: Sibylle Kazeroid | Proofreaders: David Robinson, Tracy Rothschild Lynch
Marketer: Ellen John

Manufactured in Malaysia

10 9 8 7 6 5 4 3 2 1

First Edition

Cover design: Monica Cheng
Front cover photographs (*clockwise from top left*): PA Images via Getty Images; Australia Telescope National Facility; Aflo Co. Ltd./Alamy; via Barbara Moore; Dinodia Photos/Alamy; NYPL/Interim Archives/Getty Images
Back cover photograph: Public domain

The authorized representative in the EU for product safety and compliance is Penguin Random House Ireland, Morrison Chambers, 32 Nassau Street, Dublin D02 YH68, Ireland, https://eu-contact.penguin.ie.